for Jennifer
from Elaine
— Christmas 1965

BOTTICELLI

PHAIDON

SELF-PORTRAIT OF BOTTICELLI, ABOUT 1476. Enlarged Detail from Plate 12. Florence, Uffizi

BOTTICELLI

BY LIONELLO VENTURI

WITH FIFTY PLATES IN FULL COLOUR

PUBLISHED BY THE PHAIDON PRESS

MADE IN GREAT BRITAIN

PRINTED BY HUNT BARNARD & CO · LTD · AYLESBURY · BUCKINGHAMSHIRE

BOTTICELLI

Throughout the world admiration for Botticelli is accompanied by a certain affection for the grace of his angels and his Madonnas and for the aura of melancholy surrounding all his figures. We are grateful to Botticelli for his art and wish we could comfort his grief. But the public has no conception of the difficulties criticism encounters when it attempts to interpret and appreciate the artist.

It is well known that after Botticelli's death his greatness remained unrecognized until it was rediscovered in England between 1867 and 1871 thanks to Dante Gabriele Rossetti, Swinburne, Walter Pater and Ruskin. All four felt the importance of Botticelli as a primitive and a decadent, and Pater shows clearly how great a fascination the painter must have exercised on him and his friends when he speaks of 'the peculiar sentiment with which he infuses his profane and sacred persons, comely, and in a certain sense like angels, but with a sense of displacement or loss about them – the wistfulness of exiles, conscious of a passion and energy greater than any known issue of them explains, which runs through all his varied work with a sentiment of ineffable melancholy.' Ruskin makes Botticelli, together with Fra Angelico, the representative of the Christian-Romantic school, and all his art was considered at that time as expressing a sigh of regret, a feminine languor, a kind of fantastic arbitrariness as regards reality, the manifestation of an ailing soul which finds its best expression in the gentleness of angels.

Now all this exists in Botticelli, but not this alone; and for this reason the critical reaction was salutary which dates from the beginning of our century and was promoted mainly by Horne and Mesnil. This reaction is founded on a contemporary tradition (1485–86), according to which the works of Botticelli 'have a virile air, great judgment and perfect sense of proportion'. Here, then, is another Botticelli, virile and audacious, master of all the science of his art, of all the secrets of perspective. An echo of this tradition may be found in Vasari, who saw in Botticelli's *St. Augustine* the reflection of that profound 'cogitation and most acute subtlety, generally found in persons of sense who are continually occupied with the investigation of very elevated and difficult things'. The new critical tendency therefore started from the *St. Augustine* and the realistic portraits in its endeavour to discover the 'real' Botticelli, and exalted their virile energy, their plastic relief, their realistic objectivity and moral vigour, their grand and monumental style. And while all this exists in Botticelli, it is only a partial view. To Botticelli-Angelico the critics have opposed a Botticelli-Michelangelo, and what has been left out of consideration is still Botticelli himself.

An indication, be it only a summary one, of the differences in character between the art of Botticelli and that of other fifteenth-century Florentine painters, may serve as a guide. Botticelli was the pupil of Fra Filippo Lippi. Both master and pupil had the 'appetite for beauty', that is to say their art is sensuous and at the same time transcends the senses in its endeavour to attain spiritual grace. This attainment, however, soon ceases in Lippi, whereas in Botticelli it continues on the way towards moral, ascetic and mystical grace. Botticelli was influenced by Antonio Pollaiuolo, to whom he owes the suggestion of an incisive line, realizing the anatomical construction of the bodies, their plastic strength, their physical movement so suited for expressing the impulses of their souls.

Pollaiuolo, absorbed in his energy of line, plastic form and movement, found his catharsis in 'terribilità', whereas Botticelli on the other hand never forgot to soften his line, to make it an object of contemplation, to render it serene by its rhythm. Andrea del Castagno and Andrea Verrocchio suggested to Botticelli energy of rhythm and of plastic planes, and also encouraged him in his search for a dramatic vigour, for a passionate seriousness and a monumental synthesis. Botticelli assimilated all this, but he preferred the serene repose to be found in the freshness of flowers, in the delicacies of bodies, in the gracefulness of the dance.

If we carry the comparison still further, we see that Botticelli has neither the synthetic rigour nor the monumental grandeur and moral plenitude of Masaccio; nor has he the infantile celestiality or resigned gentleness of Fra Angelico, nor the theoretical heroism, the spatial unity or chromatic harmony of Piero della Francesca. Among the achievers of physical realism, the assertors of moral energy, Botticelli seems archaic, wavering between Jove and Christ, between Venus and the Magdalen.

He knows more or less everything that was known at his time, but he perceives it only in order to dream, to sigh, to love. His road is a separate one, but he does not lag behind. Once he has given expression to his dream, all his knowledge is at his disposal. And his regrets, his dancing lines, are not a return to the faith of the Middle Ages or to the style of Gothic art: they are a presentiment of the Reformation. That is why this painter, who was behind his own times, is a precursor of the modern romantic tendency in art. If we bear all this in mind, we can understand how he was able to find room in his soul for both feminine melancholy and the 'virile air'. In fact he dreams with all the sweetness of melancholy, with a wavering faith reduced to regret, with the sadness of the exile, but the energy of his expression, the strength which enables him to impose his dream as the most real of real things, that is his 'virile air'. Feminine melancholy and virile air complete each other reciprocally and become fused as content and form are always fused in a work of art. The virile air is the form, the expressive intensity of his longings.

Botticelli's secular pictures are the most famous: the *Primavera* and the *Birth of Venus*. Ruskin has described him as the man in whom the spirit of Greece was born again. But if we examine his Venus and his Graces, we find that they have nothing in common with Greek statues; they belong to another world. Many artists, before and after him, have studied Greek statues, but he did not. To us he may appear to be a Greek by birth, in other words a cultured man and a gentleman, which he was by nature, just as the style of Greek works suggests to us what the Greeks were like. In short his Greekness is his intellectual and moral dignity. And if his paganism appears mournful, that is because Christianity did not come in vain, and in reality even the pagans could not always remain satisfied with physical enjoyment. Since the world is seen to be unknowable, the impossibility of understanding breeds sadness. The thought of youth is inseparable from the thought of death, as it was with Lorenzo de' Medici:

Who would be glad, then let him be;
Of to-morrow there's no certainty.

The Renaissance in Florence began with an absolute faith in man, in his omnipotence, in his unique beauty, and of man it made the microcosm in which the entire universe was contained. The immanence of divinity in man not only gave a new aspect to religion, but also concentrated in man, the conqueror of nature, every reasoning of science, every contemplation of art. But soon a tremor of scepticism entered into this faith, and while it induced Leonardo to seek in the universe what he could not find in man, it led Botticelli to mourn for the lost certainty of faith and to aspire towards a new belief.

Botticelli's religious pictures inspired Ruskin to call him a Reformer of the Church. Naturally the expression reformer can be used of Botticelli only in the metaphorical sense. He had not even the desire to construct for himself his own life. He studied in accordance with the wishes of his family, he did not leave his home even after attaining maturity; he had no atelier distinct from his own house and he did not found a family of his own; he painted at first for the Pope and the Medici and later he worked for the glory of Savonarola. It would be difficult to find an existence which adapted itself more completely to the exigencies of circumstances from day to day. His happy years he spent among numerous and congenial friends, his later years in silence and oblivion. He was a reformer who believed in his Church, as Ruskin says. In other words his reform never consisted in action of any kind. He continued to believe in the Church, and therefore his mind was at peace and he was able to follow in peace his dream of beauty. Nevertheless this beauty had something prophetic in it. It was the darkest moment in the history of Florence, the period which was preparing the political ruin of the city, when the Borgia Pope held sway and Savonarola was condemned to the stake. The violence of unchained passions, the display of every kind of vileness, reached its zenith. And Botticelli painted his Venuses not in an anti-Christian spirit, he painted his Madonnas not for purposes of ecclesiastical propaganda, but for his love of Christianity. Everything touched by Botticelli breathes a sense of charity, such as is rarely found throughout the centuries. His reform was in the name of the gentleness of feeling, and therefore was not outside the realm of art.

Ruskin was also the first to understand that Botticelli's vision is centred in his outlines. His preference for line as against chiaroscuro or colour is a limitation of his genius, but within that limitation it is his strength, his glory. He is one of the greatest poets of line whom history records. Antonio Pollaiuolo taught him how much artistic profit may be extracted from the outline, when it is conceived incisively, both as regards the construction of the human body in its function of relief, and in order to suggest movement, as an accentuation or impulse. Botticelli dreams fantastic arabesques, slow and continuous dance-rhythms, the gracefulness of line; and he knows how to realize them in their function of relief and movement. Nothing can take from his line its contemplative value, its fairy-like delicacy, even when it is based on natural vision. And natural vision thus becomes the form of his dream.

In general those compositions of Botticelli which contain many figures appear incoherent, lacking in unity. The multiplication of subjects in each of the frescoes in the Sistine Chapel renders the compositional unity still weaker. At this point we may recall a saying of Berenson: Botticelli prefers presentation to representation. This is true especially of his composition. The presentation of the figure, or groups of figures, realized in line, assumes such importance in Botticelli's mind that he sacrifices to it the illustrative effectiveness of the story or allegory and the relationship between the various episodes. Take, for example, the *Primavera*: our attention is drawn by the Graces, the Venus, the Mercury or the Flora; the impressiveness of their appearance is such that our interest in the allegory disappears. Even a background of flowers becomes more important than the ensemble. But we must remember that if the ensemble existed, the magical effect of the individual figures would be less intense. They would no longer emerge from mystery like the figures of a dream. Yet

7

it is possible to discover a rhythm in Botticelli's compositions: the *rhythm of detail*, which finds its justification in the very intensity with which each detail is conceived.

It is more difficult to discover the personality of Botticelli through his colouring. He had certainly a very fine feeling for the individual colours and their relationship to chiaroscuro, and some of his charming colour-schemes are unforgettable. Notwithstanding this, his vision does not appear to react to light as did that of Piero della Francesca, despite the importance which Antonio Pollaiuolo and Andrea del Castagno attached to such reactions. Botticelli preferred to follow the nuances of tints such as his first master Lippo Lippi had imagined, and sometimes he is content to add to Lippi's colour-schemes only a contribution of sporadic, though charming, inventions. Elsewhere, as, for example, in the *Primavera*, he attenuates his colours as regards both lightness and intensity, reducing them towards a general scale of greys and blues. The function of these almost neutral tones is to accompany and emphasize the melancholy expression conveyed by the linear rhythm; in other words, their character is predominantly illustrative. Botticelli thus achieves unity of colouring only by abandoning to some extent the autonomous values of the colours themselves.

In other pictures his colour-scheme plays a more important role, but it never achieves unity. His colouring, like his composition, is based on the detail. Take, for example, the *Nativity* in the National Gallery. The group of angels is depicted partly against the mystical heaven (gold ground), partly against the actual sky (blue ground). Some touches of gold are found again in the roof of the hut; the other bright colours of the draperies are set off against the dark-green background of trees and grass. But these bright colours – white, pink, blue, yellow – do not vary their tints in accordance with the variations of the background. They are delightful in their freshness, they are gems in themselves; the gold, blue or dark green are merely symbolical backgrounds from which the colours of the draperies are made to stand out boldly. This picture is a typical example of Botticelli's colouring, which conforms with the composition according to detail.

In the episodes from the life of St. Zenobius we find a new chromatic tendency. Not only do all the individual colours assume a new intensity, but their relationship with one another is based entirely on contrasts and oppositions. This does not result in a bursting forth of light, for the contrast is not one of complementary colours functioning as light and shadow. It is a contrast of tints, expressing dramatic despair with its own means. The lines and composition of the figures produce the same expression. It can no longer be said, as was the case with the *Primavera*, that the colouring is subordinated to the line. In the St. Zenobius pictures the colouring is parallel to the line and co-ordinated with it; it retains its own autonomy, however perfect the co-ordination; it has its own value, expressive and not illustrative. Death did not permit the painter to carry this happy tendency still further.

Such are the ways of approach to the understanding of Botticelli's personality. His manner of feeling is delicately feminine, but the power of his imagination gives this feeling its 'virile air'; his historical position, that is to say his attitude towards human life, urges him towards a moral reform of the Church, while a miraculous innate impulse endows all his figures with the charm of an insuperable dignity; his composition and colouring are conceived with such intensity in every detail that they do not produce an ensemble, because unity and synthesis are concentrated on the predominating element – line. It is the harmonious linear rhythm which justifies and exalts both composition and colouring, which reveals the forms and expresses the emotions. And it is for this that Botticelli creates his pictures, with an independence and elevation seldom equalled in all the history of art; for this that he draws upon his feelings, his knowledge and his will, to give to a whole world that unique aspect which is known by the name of Botticelli.

Precisely because of his peculiar sensitivity to line it is natural that he should have become one of the most brilliant draughtsmen of the Renaissance, as Vasari already realized. Few of his drawings are still in existence apart from the illustrations to the *Divine Comedy*, but each one is a complete work of art, perfect in itself even without colours (see A. Bertini, *Botticelli*, I Grandi Maestri del Disegno, Milan, 1953).

*   *   *

BOTTICELLI was born c.1445 and entered the workshop of Fra Lippo Lippi about 1459. In 1470 he painted the first of his works which we can date with certainty – the *Fortitude* now in the Uffizi, in which the influence of Antonio Pollaiuolo is apparent. In the *St. Sebastian*, which he painted in 1474 when he was barely thirty years old, he makes a gallant attempt at the nude, carefully studied in its anatomical construction, with the head inclined in sentimental fashion, to show that we have to do with a martyr. The chiaroscuro is studied with a care unusual in Botticelli's works, but for this very reason the linear rhythm is less striking.

In the *Judith*, painted shortly after 1470, the linear rhythm, on the contrary, is perfect and evident. Movement serves as pretext for the dancing outlines of the figure of Judith. In that of the maid the movement is better realized, but perhaps for this reason less poetic. Judith moves with a studied gracefulness which serves to maintain the equilibrium between the coarse movement of the maid and the rather dead immobility of the natural surroundings.

In the *Madonna of the Eucharist* another aspect of Botticelli appears in an already perfected form: the Christian symbolical aspect. In it we find plastic form achieved by means of chiaroscuro in a highly developed manner, while the undulating outlines give to the plastic forms the value of movement. But the new element in the picture is the compositional motive. Lippo Lippi had shown that it is possible to derive motives full of decorative grace and homely affection from the association of angels with the Child Christ, the mind of the beholder being thus diverted from the religious character of the representation. Botticelli returns to the religious motive with a seriousness of intention unknown to Lippo Lippi. The angel is not playing with the Child, but offering him a plate containing ears of corn and grapes, the fruits of His Passion, while the Madonna takes an ear of corn and hands it to her Son. The attention is concentrated on the symbol, and the spiritual element is constituted by the contemplation of the symbol, by the melancholy reflection on the future Passion of which the symbol is a presage, by grief for the fatal sacrifice. Just as the movement of Judith was transformed into grace, so the homage of the angel becomes contemplation of the symbol of the Passion. In other words Botticelli frees himself from all action, and aims above all things at 'presentation', though it is clear that in this case the presentation is not in opposition to the representation, but is identified with the representation of something which is not action, not the external reality, but intimate spirituality or, more simply, contemplation.

It is thus possible to detect the fundamental motives of Botticelli's art in the first five years of his already well-defined activity, between 1470 and 1475. These motives are: realistic energy giving way to sentimental aspiration, movement transformed into the grace of linear rhythm, the religious theme translated into mystical contemplation. These motives are developed in the following years and interwoven in the most varied manner. From 1475 to 1482 the realistic energy of his representation attains its maximum development, while his psychological expression is accentuated.

Two *Adorations of the Magi*, one at Florence in the Uffizi, painted about 1477, and the other in the National Gallery of Art at Washington, painted in 1481–82, show clearly how Botticelli's art developed during these years. In the Uffizi *Adoration* the realistic intention is obvious: not only is there a great abundance of portraits – and however beautiful they may be, we feel that their participation in the scene is purely relative, as supernumerary figures – but the composition also is conceived more in depth than as regards surface, the perspective space being occupied by the figures in such a way that it becomes rather artificial, especially in the series of figures on the right. The execution of the individual figures is stupendous in its dignity and gracefulness, but the ensemble remains to a certain extent limited and restricted. Physical movement and moral vigour are both lacking.

If, on the other hand, we turn to the Mellon *Adoration*, there seem to be no portraits, or at least we do not notice them. The figures are no longer supernumerary; their attitudes, even when full of dignity and grace, make them participants in the homage to God. Here too the spatial perspective is conceived in depth, but instead of being abruptly shut off it is extended towards the sky, and the superimposition of the figures is largely compensated by their distribution on the surface plane. Unity of vision is attained on the surface, as moral unity is achieved in the act of adoration. And here we understand the meaning of 'composition according to detail'. It is a kind of distribution of the surface, sometimes crowded, sometimes sparsely occupied, the rhythm of which is to be found not in unity but in succession, not in the mass but in the line.

In 1478 Botticelli was commissioned to paint the effigies of those who had been hanged for their share in the conspiracy of the Pazzi. Perhaps on that occasion he understood the importance of the art of Andrea del Castagno, who had also painted effigies of hanged criminals. However that may be, in 1480 Botticelli painted for the church of Ognissanti in Florence a *St. Augustine* with a degree of physical energy, a realistic courage and a moral enthusiasm such as he rarely displayed in all his career. The outlines are broken, the planes become masses, perspective is emphasized so that the figure may attain monumentality. A glance at the feeble realism of Ghirlandaio, who painted the companion figure of St. Jerome, is sufficient to show that Botticelli's is realism indeed, but a transcendental realism.

The three frescoes in the Sistine Chapel, painted in 1481–82 for Pope Sixtus IV, raised Botticelli to the front rank among his contemporaries and with them he achieved fame and wealth. The interest of these compositions lies in the succession of figures: the various episodes take place from right to left, and the perspective depth seems only a pretext for enriching the movement of the lines on the surface.

In the fresco of the *Youth of Moses* the centre of the composition on the first plane is provided by the scene of Moses watering the flocks of the daughters of Jethro; the suave white and blond of the two girls, in undulating attitudes as if about to dance, and the eagerness of Moses form an idyll which Botticelli chose from among these episodes certainly not on account of its significance as regards Moses, but because it was the most suited to his own imagination. In the story of Moses, the smiting of the Egyptian and the return of Moses to Egypt are the prelude and the consequence of this idyll. For Botticelli, however, they are unimportant episodes which give him an opportunity of displaying his realistic power and his dramatic energy.

FLORA. Detail from Plate 10

THE YOUTH OF MOSES. Fresco by Botticelli in the Sistine Chapel (cf. Plate 15)

Less successful, more deliberate and regulated, is the composition of the *Purification of the Leper*. The healing of leprosy is a symbol of the purification of the soul by means of faith, and has its counterpart in the Temptation of Christ represented in the background. All that is very theological, but it had not the power to quicken Botticelli's imagination. He therefore had recourse to his 'perspective science' for this composition, and felt free to create a wonderful series of portraits, and also a figure of a woman advancing with a bundle on her head which is among the finest of his female figures.

The third fresco represents *Moses and Aaron punishing Korah, Dathan and Abiram*. Botticelli found inspiration in the dramatic element of Moses' magic gesture and the despair on the faces of the condemned men, and for this reason he made this episode the centre of the composition, while the attack on Moses by Korah's band and the vengeance of Jehovah are minor episodes. Being in Rome, Botticelli wished to pay his tribute of admiration to the ancient monuments of the city and introduced the Arch of Constantine in the background. It was an absent-minded tribute and it is easy to see how the arch merely intrudes on the background and impairs the dramatic value of the Biblical scene.

After his return to Florence from Rome in 1482, and until about 1490, Botticelli received numerous commissions for both sacred and secular works. At this time the report that he was the greatest among the painters then living in Florence spread to Milan. His style during these years gained in natural facility, sureness and monumentality. We shall speak later of what it lost at the same time.

Before leaving Rome, about 1478, he painted the *Primavera* for Lorenzo di Pier Francesco de' Medici, for whom he afterwards painted the *Birth of Venus*. This Lorenzo must not be confused with Lorenzo il Magnifico. The *Primavera* shows Venus surrounded by the Graces, Mercury, Cupid, an Hour and Flora wafted by Zephyrus. Venus is conceived like a Madonna, Mercury like a St. Sebastian. The Graces however represent something new in Botticelli's art, an achievement which his genius never surpassed, one of the greatest creations in the whole of painting. Their sensibility is not Christian, but neither is it pagan. To the service of the pagan Graces Botticelli brought the secular experience of Gothic line, together with the possibility of Christian charity and piety. The result is a conception unique in history. Their beauty lies in the linear rhythm of the bodies and the veils undulating continually, yet without action. It is a prodigious incarnation of the eternal ideal of the dance.

With the exception perhaps of those of Zephyr and Flora, the presentation of the figures in this picture finds a perfect rhythm, undisturbed by the representation of action and becoming an aim in itself. This does not by any means signify that the picture lacks content, which is to be found in the depiction of youth and flowers, contemplated with a sigh of regret. But this subject-matter is well adapted to the presentation. When it is no longer there, the presentation suffers.

The *Birth of Venus*, painted about 1485, is perhaps Botticelli's most popular work. His art is now so sure of itself that it can display all he wishes and nothing more; it loses in profundity what it gains in clarity. In the movement of the winds and of the nymph there is plenty of energy, even though all action is avoided, an energy which serves as a framework for the calm, ethereal apparition of the goddess, whose timid demeanour seems to be asking pardon for her beauty, as if conscious of the modesty of the Magdalen.

More antique in inspiration are the figures in the *Pallas and the Centaur*, painted about 1488. But whether it is to be ascribed to the subject, or to a moment of abandonment to natural facility, the fact remains that in this picture the personality of Botticelli is veiled; it appears indifferent in the figure of Pallas and is scarcely visible except in the features of the Centaur, which, instead of being a monster of violence, rages impotently like an unhappy Moses.

Botticelli's portraits, as has already been noted, are generally inferior to the figures he painted in his episodes. Probably his imaginative faculty needed movement in order to find its sovereign rhythm, and the bust-length portrait, as conceived by the Quattrocento, was unable to provide this. Then again, we must remember the transcendental character of Botticelli's realism. Whatever the reason may be, his so-called 'Simonettas' are not of the same quality as his Graces, while of his male portraits only the Lorenzano, with the vital energy of its sitter, and a portrait of a young man in the National Gallery which is an exceptional expression of affection, can be counted among the great masterpieces of our artist.

On his return from Rome Botticelli executed several great pictures of a religious character, among them various *tondi*, in which his feeling for the distribution of form on the surface was able to manifest itself successfully. The *Magnificat* is the most famous of these, despite its bad state of preservation; and in fact the compositional skill shown in this *tondo* is unique. Nevertheless it is legitimate to suppose that the weakening of the intensity of meditation, as compared with the *Madonna of the Eucharist*, may be due not only to restoration but also to facile execution. Such facility must be classed as conventional, and can be found exaggerated beyond all limits in works of Botticelli's school, though it can also be discerned in some of the pictures by his own hand, as, for example, in the *Madonna with the Pomegranate*.

The masterpiece among Botticelli's large religious compositions is undoubtedly the *St. Barnabas Altar-piece*, painted immediately after his return from Rome. In this painting the intensity of execution has resulted in several stupendous figures: the St. Catherine, so much more vital than Venus because she betrays her inward emotion; the St. Barnabas; an angel with the symbols of martyrdom; and above all John the Baptist, one of the most profound and human figures ever created by an artist. Here we perceive how the deepest abysses of torment and pain may be expressed with artistic gracefulness.

If we compare the Baptist in this picture with that in the Santo Spirito altar-piece, we perceive how great is the difference between the creation of genius and the clever figure of the artisan, even though both may be identified with the name of Botticelli. It should be noted, too, that the Santo Spirito altar-piece is one of Botticelli's most successful compositions; but successful composition, the skilful distribution of the figures and the placing of each of them in a leafy pergola, as well as the correct drawing and proportions of the figures, all these things were the work of Botticelli the artisan, admirable work without a doubt, but not the greatest, the most profound, in short not the pure artistic element in his complex personality.

In the large *Coronation of the Virgin*, painted in 1490, a new tonality appears. Whereas between 1484 and 1488 a certain self-satisfaction is perceptible in Botticelli's works, a certain reliance on his own skill, in the *Coronation* a tremor of anxiety, of anguish and new aspirations, is revealed. The emotion of the angels is transformed into a harsher grace, the faith of St. Jerome assumes a new certitude and dignity. In addition to this we note a certain departure from the 'perfect sense of proportion' (for which reason this painting has not found favour with the critics), an agitation which is not without grandeur in its intense inwardness, an intensity of colouring which seeks to make itself independent of chiaroscuro.

Other works by Botticelli also reveal this intensification of his art, this need for drama, which hitherto has not been adequately appreciated by any critic save Adolfo Venturi. One such work is the so-called *Derelitta*. The subject is perhaps of Biblical inspiration. But here too the historical fact is completely surpassed by the eternally human interpretation.

The *Annunciation* is a theme well suited for the idyll, and Botticelli painted several pictures of the subject idyllically. But when about 1490 he painted the *Annunciation* now in the Uffizi, the idyllic element disappeared. The earnestness of the angelic messenger and the reaction of the Madonna impart a melancholy air to the episode. Even the colours are more severe, and the chiaroscuro becomes summary in order to give more relief to the outlines and movement. For this reason workshop collaboration has been assumed for this picture, though in reality it is merely an intensification of expression at the expense of abstract technique.

The *Calumny of Apelles* was painted after 1490; the subject of the picture is derived from Lucian and Alberti. Fifteen years before Botticelli had been unable to perceive the classicality of Venus, and now he is still unable to imagine that of Apelles. But whereas fifteen years before he had abandoned himself to the dream of grace originating in his Christian sensibility, in the *Calumny* he is tormented by the spectacle of human vileness and the suffering caused thereby. His lines no longer dance, but leap. This does not mean that beauty vanishes; on the contrary it is refined, based on dramatic contrasts with ugliness, and becomes moral beauty.

In 1492 Lorenzo il Magnifico died, and in 1498 Savonarola was burned at the stake. One of Savonarola's followers, Simone Filipepi, has left us an account of how his brother Alessandro, that is to say Botticelli, collected the proofs of the frate's innocence. The inscription on the *Nativity* in London, painted in 1500, informs us that Botticelli interpreted the death of Savonarola as the moment of the unloosing of the demon according to the Apocalypse, and expressed the hope that the demon would be thrown into chains again. Even without this documentary proof, anyone can find in Botticelli's paintings a thousand reasons in support of the tradition handed down by Vasari, that Botticelli became a follower of Savonarola. The moral and religious intensification of his last works is obvious to everybody and assumed a dramatic form because Botticelli, like Savonarola, felt that the demon had been unloosed during the Papacy of Alexander Borgia. Moreover this earnestness of moral and religious life had been present in Botticelli ever since, many years before, he had transformed the domestic motive of the Lippesque tradition into the mystical contemplation of the *Madonna of the Eucharist*.

In the *Nativity* the spirit of piety, of compassion for the fate of mankind, dominates the picture. The angels still dance against the gold background, but their gracefulness has acquired a melancholy element. The adoration of the new-born Child is no longer a motive for joy; the sense of human guilt weighs too heavily on the shoulders of the adorers, who are bent beneath their grief. Even the rejoicing of the angels with mankind liberated at last from the demon is too constrained to be joyful.

In the *Crucifixion* in the Fogg Museum, the mystical anguish of the Magdalen, who throws herself in despair at the foot of the Cross, is one of the highest achievements of art. In the background is Florence, and it may be that the angel is an allegorical representation of the punishment of the city for the burning of Savonarola; but the desperate attitude of the Magdalen is not an allegorical representation; here the mystical ascension coincides with the artistic creation.

Of the colouring of the episodes from the life of St. Zenobius we have already spoken. One must try to imagine lines as crude as the contrasts of the tints, a simplification of the masses by means of unity of gesture in the groups, and above all the evidence of the despair which filled the artist's soul. His sensibility has not become blunted, it has been transformed into moral conscience. And on his conscience burst the drama of that corruption against which the Reformation was soon to array itself.

In 1510 Botticelli died in seclusion and in silence, according to Vasari. But Vasari failed to understand that isolation was necessary to the artist's spiritual life. He was able to find, even on earth, the salvation of his soul, the last touch to make his mortal figure appear to us as perfect as the image of his art. So that, if in our minds we traverse once again the course of Botticelli's art, we perceive that from his earliest youth, even from birth, he brought with him a new element of grace and charity. The grace enabled him to give transcendental value to his realism; the charity introduced a human emotion in the midst of physical beauty. The *Judith*, the *Madonna of the Eucharist*, the two *Adorations of the Magi*, the *Primavera*, the *St. Augustine*, the frescoes in the Sistine Chapel, the St. Barnabas altar-piece, all suggest the grace and generous impulses of convictions and dreams; there follows a period of fulfilment, of external perfection, which we can never weary of admiring, but which we feel at the end contains less of the real Botticelli: *Venus and Mars*, the *Birth of Venus*, *Pallas and the Centaur*, the Santo Spirito altar-piece. But face to face with the danger that he himself would become too superficial, he understood the danger, to which the whole of humanity is exposed, of losing its soul. Botticelli is torn by anguish and emotion, he becomes more complicated and succeeds in creating moral beauty: the '*Derelitta*', the *Annunciation*, the *Coronation*, the *Calumny of Apelles*. After the death of Savonarola comes despair, and meditating on his own despair he expresses his emotion in the *Nativity*, and creates the sorrowful accents of the *Crucifixion* and of the episodes from the life of St. Zenobius. In this way the trajectory is accomplished, from the idyllic fantasy of the sensuous young man to the magnanimous wrath of the seer.

*　　*　　*

THE foregoing essay was written in 1937 and since then there have been important contributions to our understanding of Botticelli: Sergio Bettini, *Botticelli*, Bergamo, 1942; E. H. Gombrich, *Botticelli's Mythologies: A Study in the Neoplatonic Symbolism of his Circle*, Journal of the Warburg and Courtauld Institutes, London, 1945; Pierre Francastel, *Peinture et Société: Naissance et Destruction d'un Espace Plastique de la Renaissance au Cubisme*, Lyon, 1951; Giulio Carlo Argan, *Botticelli*, Geneva 1957.

Sergio Bettini emphasizes certain of the artist's characteristics: his hesitation between space and decoration, between a blend or a contrast of colour, between ardour and melancholy, sensuality and purity: his need to isolate the figure by making it the focus of attention: his desire to adhere to the medieval tradition even in the conception of the *Birth of Venus* as a triptych; the more opaque chromatic material of the later works.

Pierre Francastel cites Botticelli as the most obvious proof that the spatial system elaborated by Alberti was not followed by all the artists of the second half of the Quattrocento. Botticelli's *Primavera* 'nous offre l'exemple de plusieurs épisodes groupés dans un espace aussi peu unitaire que possible, aussi peu réel qu'on peut l'imaginer, dans un espace symbolique où les figures et le fond ne sont pas vus sous le même angle. C'est bien davantage l'espace plural et cubique déduit à travers le giottisme d'une interprétation de la scène antico-médiévale que l'espace ouvert et unitaire de Brunelleschi qui triomphe' (p. 59). Given the distinction between mythical and geometric thought,

Francastel stresses the mythical value and the symbolical significance of the Birth of Venus within the Neo-Platonic circle.

Gombrich is concerned to provide the historical documentation of the style critics' intuitive perceptions. The *Primavera* was painted for Lorenzo di Pierfrancesco de'Medici, a cousin but not a close friend of Lorenzo the Magnificent. Now, a letter written in 1477–78 by Marsilio Ficino to the youthful Lorenzo di Pierfrancesco outlines the mode of life best suited to him in the future. And amongst the qualities required of him the most important is the one exemplified by Venus, i.e. Humanity (Humanitas) whose soul and mind are Love and Charity, whose eyes are Dignity and Magnanimity, etc. It is a horoscope and at the same time a set of moral precepts which Ficino hopes young Lorenzo will learn by heart. In 1477 the Villa di Castello was purchased by Lorenzo and instead of hanging it with tapestries he asked Botticelli to paint his *Primavera* in accordance with the ideas of Ficino, who set great store by visual education. While planning the subject-matter of the painting Ficino and his friends, all intimates of Lorenzo di Pierfrancesco, drew on Apuleius and his description of Venus. Thus Venus appears in the centre of the picture between on the one hand the dancing Graces and Mercury, who symbolizes Paris and his mission of favour towards Venus, and on the other side one of the Hours, Botticelli's simplification of the several Hours indicated by Apuleius. Similarly a single Cupid hovers above Venus instead of several. On the right the Hour is balanced by Flora and Zephyr. The abundance of flowers, Venus' relaxed pose with the head slightly bent, are suggested by Apuleius. Thus the subject of the picture would seem to be Venus surrounded by her court waiting to encounter Paris. Gombrich discusses the importance exercised by Ficino's writings and by Platonic allegories on the artistic result of Botticelli's work and shows how they transformed the traditional profane subjects precisely by means of the spiritual sublimity of the figures which partake both of the Christian and the pagan, in accordance with Ficino and the Neoplatonism of the period.

On the other hand the connexion between Botticelli and Lorenzo di Pierfrancesco seems un-interrupted. Their taste is opposed to the realism of Lorenzo the Magnificent, who prefers Ghirlandaio and Bertoldo, and their morality leads them to Savonarola who refers to Lorenzo di Pierfrancesco with the utmost respect and to whom Ficino himself was not hostile.

Not only the *Primavera* but also other paintings of Botticelli's are explicable by Ficino's writings: the *Villa Lemmi Frescoes* now in the Louvre, *Venus and Mars*, *Minerva and the Centaur*. Minerva, the divine Wisdom, resolves the conflict between the sensual and the intellectual as symbolized by the centaur. Similarly the *Birth of Venus* is regarded by Ficino as a cosmogonic mystery. And to under-stand the importance of Ficino's influence as an inspiration for works of art it is sufficient to recall that both Dürer and Titian had recourse to him.

Undoubtedly the iconographical interpretation of some of Botticelli's masterpieces advanced by Gombrich makes it possible to define clearly the moral and intellectual basis of Botticelli's art.

Giulio Carlo Argan widens the interpretation of Botticelli's art so as to include the whole in-tellectual climate of Florence towards the end of the Quattrocento. It is the crisis of the great systems of plastic art elaborated during the first half of the century, the crisis in the conception of space and perspective, of form as knowledge and representation of nature, of *historia* intended as a dramatic representation of human actions, of the moral and religious character of art. Art, like Ficino's philosophy, tends towards beauty, it is the means whereby all beauty is attained and an acquired awareness of the autonomy of ethics, whereby 'vanità' is condemned by Savonarola. Despite its spiritual aspirations Botticelli's religion remains indeterminate, a kind of lay religion which loves nature but transforms it by idealizing it, that Platonic love which had already appeared in the *dolce stil novo* and in Petrarch. Renouncing the rendering of objects in space, and in contrast to his almost exact contemporary, Leonardo da Vinci, Botticelli prefers to paint ideas; he creates figures, names, words, and so comes near to poetry. The figures in *Primavera* are beautiful because they are deprived of their physical solidity by a mysterious process which transforms them from natural objects to representations. Ficino maintained that beauty was something incorporeal. Instead of seeking his inspiration in nature, Botticelli seeks it in learning – Ficino, Alberti – hence the allegorical value of his figures in which are united the antique and the Christian, a union to which, however, all humanism always tended. In the later works Botticelli's style is influenced by his rejection of the humanist mythology, of the demonic ambiguity of his figures, and by a desire to stiffen his figures by accentuating and dramatizing their expression.

Thus two types of Botticelli art criticisms are synthesized by Argan: the data of formal analysis and the available information about Botticelli's own culture and the thought of his time.

Woodcut by Cristoforo Coriolano, from Vasari's *Vite*, 1568

PLATES

PLATES

1. MADONNA GUIDI. Paris, Louvre

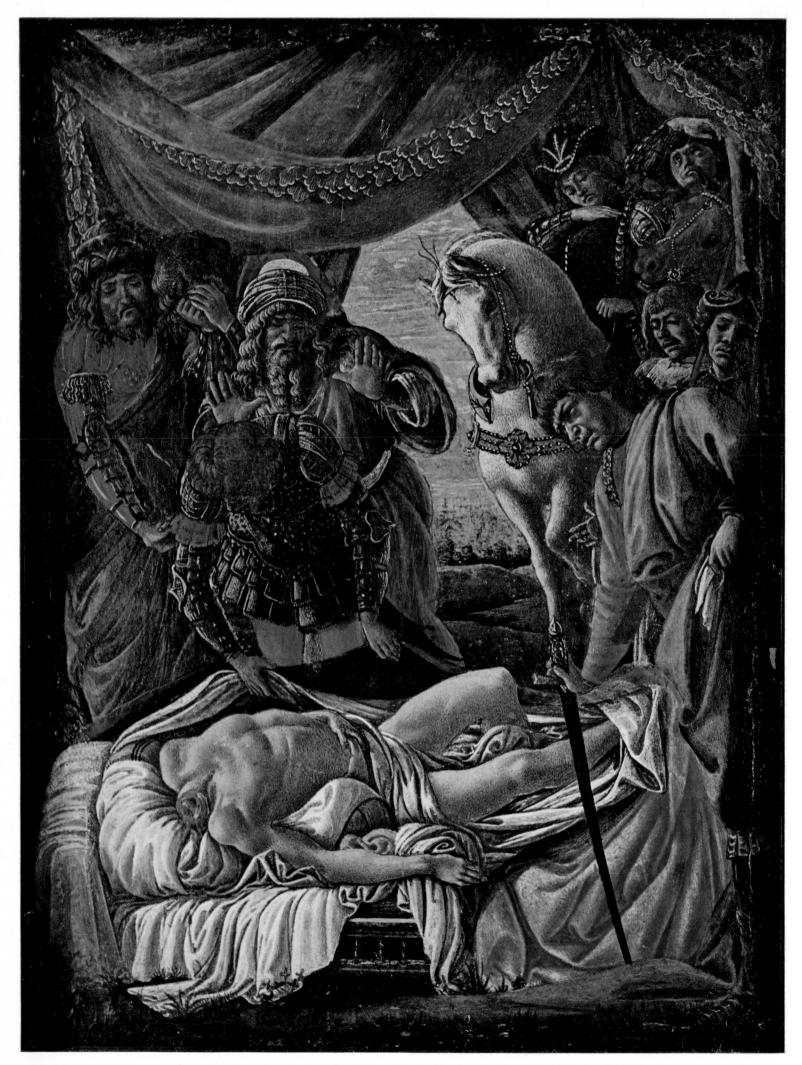

2. The Finding of the Body of Holofernes. Florence, Uffizi

3. The Return of Judith. Florence, Uffizi

4. FORTITUDE. 1470. Florence, Uffizi

5. St. Sebastian. 1474. Berlin, Museum

6. PORTRAIT OF A YOUNG MAN. Detail. London, National Gallery

7. PORTRAIT OF A YOUNG MAN. Detail. Florence, Uffizi

8. PORTRAIT OF GIULIANO DE' MEDICI. Washington, National Gallery of Art, Samuel H. Kress Collection

9. THE MADONNA OF THE EUCHARIST. Boston, Isabella Stewart Gardner Museum

10. PRIMAVERA. Florence, Uffizi

11. VENUS. Detail from Plate 10

12. The Adoration of the Magi. Florence, Uffizi

13. St. Augustine in his Cell. Fresco, 1480. Florence, Ognissanti

14. THE ARCHANGEL GABRIEL. Part of the S. Martino fresco, 1481. Florence, Belvedere

15. TWO GIRLS. Detail from the fresco "The Youth of Moses". 1481–82. Rome, Sistine Chapel

16. LANDSCAPE. Detail from the fresco "The Punishment of Korah, Dathan and Abiram". 1481–82. Rome, Sistine Chapel

17. GROUP OF ONLOOKERS. Detail from the fresco "The Purification of the Leper". 1481–82. Rome, Sistine Chapel

18. The Adoration of the Magi. 1482. Washington, National Gallery of Art, Mellon Collection

19. A Scene from Boccaccio. Part of the wall panelling of a bridal chamber. 1483. Madrid, Prado

20. AUTUMN OR ABUNDANCE. Drawing. London, British Museum

21. MINERVA AND THE CENTAUR. Florence, Uffizi

22. Venus presenting a Young Man to the Liberal Arts. Fresco. Paris, Louvre

24. HEAD OF "ASTRONOMY". Detail from Plate 22

25. HEAD OF THE BRIDE. Detail from Plate 23

26. MADONNA OF THE "MAGNIFICAT". Florence, Uffizi

27. HEAD OF THE MADONNA. Detail from Plate 26

28. Mars and Venus. London, National Gallery

29. The Birth of Venus. Florence, Uffizi

30. VENUS. Detail from Plate 29

31. Virgin and Child.
Detail from Plate 32

32. Virgin and Child with the two Saints John. 1485. Berlin, Museum

33. MADONNA WITH THE POMEGRANATE. Florence, Uffizi

34. HEAD OF THE MADONNA.
Detail from Plate 33

35. DANTE. Cologny-Geneva, Dr. Martin Bodmer collection

36. Illustration to Dante's "Divine Comedy". Tempera on parchment. Berlin, Print Room

38. MADONNA UNDER A BALDACHIN. Milan, Biblioteca Ambrosiana

39. ST. AUGUSTINE IN HIS CELL. Florence, Uffizi

40. THE ANNUNCIATION. 1490. Florence, Uffizi

41. Pietà. Milan, Poldi-Pezzoli Museum

42. THE CALUMNY OF APELLES. Florence, Uffizi

43. The Tragedy of Lucretia. Boston, Isabella Stewart Gardner Museum

44. MYSTIC NATIVITY. 1501. London, National Gallery

45. THE AGONY IN THE GARDEN. Granada, Royal Chapel

46. Judith. Amsterdam, Rijksmuseum

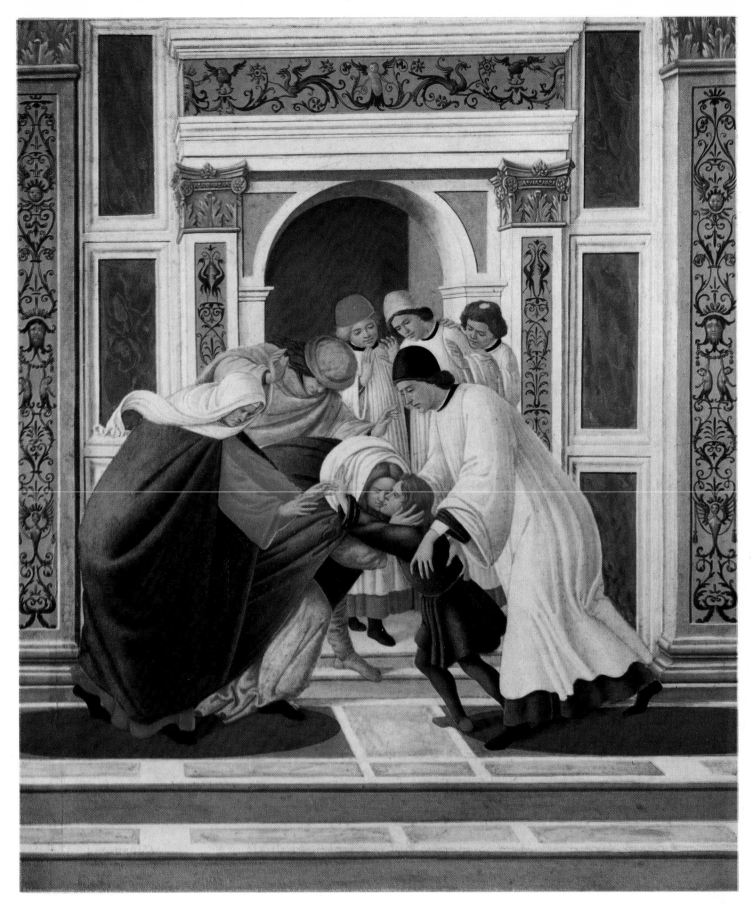

47. A MIRACLE OF ST. ZENOBIUS. Detail. Dresden, Gallery

48. A MIRACLE OF ST. ZENOBIUS. Detail. London, National Gallery

NOTES ON THE PLATES

NOTES ON THE PLATES

THE FOLLOWING NOTES ARE BY LUDWIG GOLDSCHEIDER

WHO ALSO SELECTED THE ILLUSTRATIONS

1. *Madonna Guidi*. Panel, $28\frac{3}{4}\times19\frac{1}{4}$ in. Paris, Louvre.
Attributed to Botticelli by Adolfo Venturi, Bode, Mesnil, Berenson, Salvini and other scholars, and dated from his early period, about 1468, when he was still in the workshop of Fra Filippo Lippi. Bode (1926) and Pudelko (1936) suggest that a *Madonna* by Filippo Lippi in the Munich Gallery (No. 647) may have been Botticelli's model. Lionello Venturi also accepts now (letter of April 1961) the attribution of the *Madonna Guidi* to Botticelli, but does not regard it as identical with the picture that was sold in 1902 as No. 581 of the collection of Conte Guidi da Faenza. The picture was bequeathed to the Louvre by Baron Schlichting in 1915.

2–3. *Judith and Holofernes*. Two panels, each $12\frac{1}{4}\times9\frac{7}{8}$ in. Florence, Uffizi.
According to Raffaello Borghini (*Riposo*, 1584), the two panels were originally in a single frame, forming a kind of diptych. In style they depend, as Horne was the first to point out, from embroideries by Pollaiuolo (1466–70; Florence, Opera del Duomo). Plate 2 is well preserved, but in Plate 3 the servant's face and the lower part of her dress have been overpainted by a much later hand. The extent of this overpainting is shown by an old copy (formerly in the Bardini Collection, Florence), in which the lower part of the servant's dress is shaped like Turkish breeches and both her shoes are visible.
The same subject occupied Botticelli also in later years: see the figure of Judith at the far right of Plate 42; the relief above this figure shows the "Death of Holofernes", and the relief underneath "Judith's Return to Bethulia".

4. *Fortitude*. Panel, $65\frac{3}{4}\times34\frac{1}{4}$ in. Florence, Uffizi.
This is the earliest documented painting by Botticelli; it belongs to a series of the *Seven Virtues* painted in 1470 for the *Tribunale di Mercancia*, the commercial court of Florence. Six of the panels (now also in the Uffizi) were painted by Piero Pollaiuolo, partly from drawings of his brother Antonio; the seventh panel is the *Fortitude*, for which Botticelli received payment on August 18, 1470. It seems very probable that Verrocchio also took part in the competition for this order: a drawing from his workshop for the figure of *Faith* is still extant (Van Marle xi, fig. 318). Verrocchio's influence can be recognized in Botticelli's *Fortitude*, particularly in the drawing of the armour.
The seven paintings of the Virtues were originally let into the panelling above the bench on which the six magistrates of the court used to sit. The perspective of the pictures allows for the fact that they were intended for "high hanging" – with their top about twelve feet above the floor – and this explains why the throne seems to fall back.
Although better preserved than the other pictures of the series, the *Fortitude* is damaged in many parts. Retouching can be recognized particularly in the right half of the face, on the neck and on the right hand.

5. *St. Sebastian*. Panel, $76\frac{3}{4}\times29\frac{1}{2}$ in. Berlin-Dahlem, Museum.
According to the Anonimo Gaddiano (ed. Frey, p. 105), the picture was painted in January 1474 for the Church of S. Maria Maggiore in Florence. It came to Berlin in 1821 from the Solly collection in England. Solly had attributed it erroneously to Antonio Pollaiuolo, whose influence is indeed obvious. The style of the landscape was imitated later by Botticelli's pupil, Filippino Lippi (cf. the landscape in Plate 40).
In the background, left, a meaningful episode: the departing soldiers continue their cruelty, although they find no better victims than the birds high in the air.
The picture is very well preserved.

6. *Portrait of a Young Man*. Panel, $14\frac{3}{4}\times11\frac{1}{8}$ in. London, National Gallery.
Detail in original size. See the reproduction of the complete painting on page 73.
Very well preserved.

7. *Portrait of a Young Man*. Panel, $22\frac{5}{8}\times17\frac{3}{8}$ in. Florence, Uffizi.
Detail, about $\frac{3}{4}$ original size. See the reproduction of the complete painting on page 73.
A round hole has been cut into the wooden panel on which the picture is painted, and the medal, a cast in gilt plaster, has been inserted. The medal represents Cosimo de' Medici and this has led to the assumption that the sitter was someone closely connected with the Medici family, e.g. the philosopher Pico della Mirandola, a friend of Lorenzo de' Medici; or a member of the family (either Giovanni, 1421–63, or Piero di Lorenzo, 1471–1503); or the artist who made the medal. Bode believed, wrongly, that the picture was not a work by Botticelli, but a self-portrait of the medallist Niccolò Fiorentino (1430–1514).
The landscape background, sketched in loosely in light colours, may not have been completely finished. The picture is fairly well preserved; but there are retouches on the left cheek, on the neck and particularly on the hands.

8. *Portrait of Giuliano de' Medici*. Panel, $29\frac{3}{4}\times20\frac{5}{8}$ in. Washington, National Gallery of Art, Samuel H. Kress Collection.
Several versions exist of this portrait, all of them apparently painted in Botticelli's workshop. The version in Washington

is the best. That in the Thyssen Collection, Lugano, published by Roger Fry as the original, represents Giuliano turned to the left and with open eyes; thus it differs from the other versions, but is related to Giuliano's portrait in the *Adoration of the Magi* (Plate 12). Morelli and Horne favoured the portrait in Bergamo, Bode and Yashiro that in Berlin, Venturi, Gamba and Valentiner that in Milan, Bettini and Suida that in Washington, which Berenson, too, finally accepted as an autograph work by Botticelli, though he regarded also the versions in Bergamo and Lugano as very fine.

Bettini was probably wrong in believing that the portrait in the Kress Collection had been painted during the lifetime of Giuliano (who was killed in the Pazzi conspiracy of 1478). These portraits, except that in Lugano, are based on a death-mask (as has been pointed out repeatedly): hence the rigidity of the features and the seam running from the forehead to the chin. According to Vasari, such death-masks were produced in Verrocchio's workshop. – The turtle-dove at the lower left is a symbol of mourning.

9. *Madonna of the Eucharist.* Panel, $33\frac{7}{8} \times 25\frac{5}{8}$ in. Boston, Isabella Stewart Gardner Museum.

This picture was discovered by Morelli in the summer of 1899 in a dark corner of the palace of Prince Chigi in Rome. It is the finest work of Botticelli's early period and is well preserved.

Ears of corn and grapes, bread and wine, symbolize the body and blood of Christ (Luke, xxii, 19).

10–11. *Spring (La Primavera).* Panel, 80×123 in. Florence, Uffizi.

The picture was owned by Lorenzo and Giovanni di Pierfrancesco de' Medici, the cousins of Lorenzo Magnifico; by inheritance it came into the collection of the Grand-Dukes of Tuscany.

While the poetry of this picture reveals itself to every beholder, its interpretation has remained problematic. All earlier attempts were examined and critically commented by E. H. Gombrich (*Botticelli's Mythologies: A Study in the Neoplatonic Symbolism of his Circle*, in "Journal of the Warburg and Courtauld Institutes", viii, 1945). Warburg had suggested the title "The Realm of Venus". Gombrich has added his own well-considered explanations, which are based upon a passage in the fable of Apuleius and upon a letter written by the humanist Marsilio Ficino. But attempts to interpret the picture still continue to be made: Ernesta Battista explains it as "The Round of the Four Seasons", with Zephyr (at the right, embracing Flora) representing February, and Mercury (with raised wand chasing a cloud from the trees or reaching for a fruit) representing September. According to Gombrich, the central figure, above whom Cupid hovers blindfold with a flaming arrow, is Venus-Humanitas. The group of three women in diaphanous garments, at Mercury's right, represents the three Graces (or alternatively three Horae, whom Flora in her transparent garment, joins as fourth). The ripe golden fruits, reminiscent of the apples in the Garden of the Hesperides, contradict the traditional title "La Primavera". The painting is very well preserved, but cleaning would brighten the colours in the darker parts.

12. *The Adoration of the Magi.* Panel, $43\frac{3}{4} \times 53\frac{3}{4}$ in. Florence, Uffizi.

Documents published by Jacques Mesnil (in 1903) show that the picture was commissioned from Botticelli by Giovanni Lami, a Florentine merchant, for a chapel in Santa Maria Novella. According to Gamba, the third figure from the left in the foreground is a portrait of Lami. Among the groups of spectators Botticelli has portrayed several members of the Medici family and since Vasari's time efforts have been made to identify them. The figure kneeling before the Virgin is Cosimo de' Medici; the group on the right includes Giuliano (in profile) and, below the Virgin, Piero, the father of Lorenzo Magnifico. The two at the far left have been said to be portraits of Lorenzo Magnifico and Poliziano. Some of the portraits are certainly posthumous. The figure in the yellow cloak, at the far right, is almost generally regarded as a self-portrait of Botticelli.

The original marble frame of the picture is now lost. The painting has been cut at both sides and a narrow strip is missing at the top. But in general it is well preserved, apart from slight damages at the top and left.

13. *St. Augustine in his Cell.* Fresco, $59\frac{7}{8} \times 44\frac{1}{8}$ in. Florence, Church of Ognissanti.

Commissioned by a member of the Vespucci family in 1480 as pendant to a *St. Jerome* by Ghirlandaio.

The fresco is much damaged; the columns at the sides have been newly painted by a later hand; but the principal parts, the head and hands of the saint, are well preserved.

14. *The Archangel Gabriel.* Part of a fresco, about 90×75 in. Florence, Museum Forte del Belvedere.

Left half of an *Annunciation*. The complete fresco has a size of 96×216 in. The right half is much less well preserved (see the reproduction on page 76).

According to documents published by Poggi, Botticelli painted this fresco in April and May 1481, shortly before his departure for Rome, on the wall of an open loggia of the Church of Santa Maria della Scala. In 1920 the fresco was detached from the wall and taken to the Uffizi for a restoration, which was not completed until 1952.

The damages which the fresco has suffered are clearly visible in the reproduction. At present it is – like many other frescoes detached from the walls of Florentine churches and palaces – on permanent exhibition in the Forte del Belvedere.

15–17. *Details from Botticelli's three frescoes in the Sistine Chapel* of the Vatican in Rome, 1481–82. (See the illustrations on pages 12, 74–75.) The Sistine Chapel was built under Pope Sixtus IV in 1473–81, and in the following decades was decorated with frescoes, the latest of which is Michelangelo's *Last Judgement* on the altar wall (on which Perugino's earlier paintings had to be destroyed).

A document published by Steinmann shows that on October 27, 1481, Perugino, Cosimo Rosselli, Ghirlandaio and Botticelli undertook to paint ten pictures on the walls of the Sistine Chapel and finish them by March 15, 1482 at the latest. At the time of this contract, each of the four painters had already completed one fresco. Botticelli, who had probably arrived in Rome in June 1481, had painted one of these; there can be little doubt that this was *The Purification of the Leper* (Plate 17). At that time, the portraits of Popes in the Sistine Chapel had also been completed, seven of them from designs by Botticelli. In the late autumn of 1481, Signorelli, Pinturicchio and Piero di Cosimo joined the artists working on the frescoes in the Chapel. (The last-named had an assistant, Biagio Tucci, who is probably identical with a Biagio d'Antonio da Firenze, and who later, about 1483–87, worked as Botticelli's assistant in Florence.)

The frescoes on the right-hand wall – seen from the entrance – represent the Life of Christ, those on the left-hand wall The Life of Moses. Each of Botticelli's three frescoes occupies a space of $10\frac{1}{2} \times 16\frac{1}{2}$ ft. – In August 1482, or somewhat earlier, Botticelli returned to Florence. Like all other frescoes in the Sistine Chapel, those by Botticelli have been considerably damaged and restored. The details reproduced on Plates 15–17 show parts that are relatively well preserved.

18. *The Adoration of the Magi.* 1482. Panel, 28×41 in. Washington, National Gallery of Art, Mellon Collection.
This *Adoration* is generally identified with the picture which, according to the Anonimo Gaddiano (about 1542), Botticelli painted in Rome. This enables us to date the picture, but it was probably not completed until after Botticelli's return to Florence.
This well preserved painting is an important work of Botticelli's middle period. It was given to the National Gallery of Art in 1937 by Andrew W. Mellon, who had acquired it from the Hermitage in Leningrad.

19. *A Scene from Boccaccio.* 1483. Panel, $32\frac{1}{4} \times 54\frac{3}{8}$ in. Madrid, Prado (from the Cambò Collection).
Vasari informs us that Botticelli painted a series of four pictures for the Casa Pucci. There the pictures remained until 1868 when they were sold to an English collector. The four panels illustrate the Story of Nastagio degli Onesti (*Decamerone*, fifth day, eighth Novel). Three of the panels are now in the Prado, the fourth is in the Oliver Watney Collection at Charlbury. The execution is due in part to an assistant of Botticelli's, usually identified with Bartolommeo di Giovanni. (I believe that in the first and second panels the collaboration of Biagio d'Antonio can be recognized.)
Plate 19 shows the second scene of the cycle. Driven by grief over unrequited love, Nastagio has fled into the pine forest near Ravenna (the young man at the left, raising his hands in amazement); there he sees an apparition: the ghost of a knight pursues the ghost of a girl, for whose sake he has committed suicide and been damned. In the centre of the picture, the pursuit of the girl is shown in the background, and in the foreground the knight tearing out the girl's

heart and throwing it to his dogs. According to Oskar Fischel, the riderless horse repeats the motif of Verrocchio's Colleoni model, which had been completed in 1481, before Botticelli's departure for Rome.
Later on, Botticelli represented the story of Nastagio degli Onesti once more, in three painted reliefs of the hall in the *Calumny of Apelles* (Plate 42, left upper corner, lower row, inside the arch).
It used to be thought that the four pictures had been painted for the wedding of Pierfrancesco Bini and Lucrezia Pucci in 1487; Horne has proved, however, that they were commissioned on the occasion of the wedding of Giannozzo Pucci and Lucrezia Bini in 1483. After long hesitation, Berenson also finally accepted this later date.

20. *Autumn* or *Abundance.* Allegorical drawing, $12\frac{1}{2} \times 10$ in. London, British Museum.
Pink prepared paper, pen and brown ink and faint brown wash over black chalk heightened with white.
This is Botticelli's finest drawing. Various dates have been proposed; Horne dates it about 1482.
The principal figure seems to have been influenced by Donatello's "Dovizia" (destroyed in the eighteenth century), which carried a cornucopia and stood in the old market-place of Florence. The drawing was used for a picture representing "Autumn" (Knoedler, New York; formerly Lord Rosebery, London) which was painted by some assistant in Botticelli's workshop.

21. *Minerva and the Centaur.* Canvas, $81\frac{1}{2} \times 58\frac{1}{4}$ in. Florence, Uffizi.
Painted for Lorenzo and Giovanni di Pierfrancesco de' Medici. The allegory probably represents the victory of reason over sensuality, but this interpretation fails to explain such details as Minerva's large halberd, the Centaur's bow, the overhanging rock which appears to enclose a cave, or the fence on the sea shore. Minerva's dress is embroidered with diamond rings, the emblem of Lorenzo Magnifico, and it has therefore been suggested that a homage to him is concealed in this allegory.
The picture is not well preserved. The original pigments have flaked off in many places and there is extensive damage in the forehead and the right eye of the Centaur. Many stains in the face of Minerva and elsewhere were overpainted during a recent restoration (after 1950).

22–25. *The allegorical frescoes from the Villa Lemmi.* $93\frac{1}{4} \times 106$ in. and $83\frac{1}{2} \times 111\frac{3}{4}$ in. Paris, Louvre.
In 1873, the two badly damaged frescoes, in a villa owned by Dr. Petronio Lemmi (two miles outside Florence), were freed from whitewash, then detached from the wall and in 1881 they were sold to the Louvre. While being detached, they suffered further damage.
Ulrich Thieme already declared it to be impossible that Lorenzo Tornabuoni and his bride Giovanna degli Albizzi were portrayed here. Gombrich has shown it to be most doubtful that the villa of Dr. Lemmi had ever been owned by the Tornabuoni family. – A third fresco, which has

Fig. 1. *Botticelli's Self-Portrait* (?). Detail from "The Adoration of the Magi", Uffizi, Florence, Plate 12.

Fig. 2. *Head of a Man*. Silverpoint drawing, attributed to Botticelli, or sometimes to Piero del Pollaiuolo. Rennes, Museum.

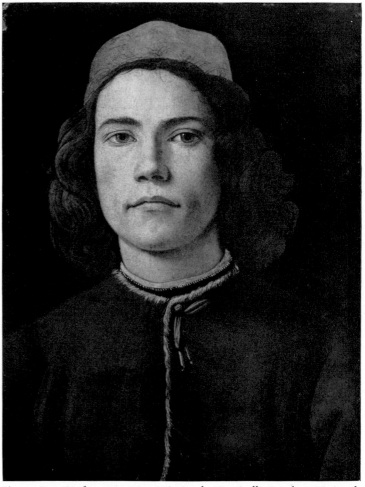

Fig. 3. *Man holding a Medal*. Painting by Botticelli. Florence, Uffizi (cf. Plate 7).

Fig. 4. *Portrait of a young Man*. Painting by Botticelli, London, National Gallery (cf. Plate 6).

Fig. 5. The Sistine Chapel, part of a wall with Botticelli's fresco *The Youth of Moses* (cf. Plate 15).

Fig. 6. *The Punishment of Korah, Dathan and Abiram*. Fresco by Botticelli in the Sistine Chapel (cf. Plate 16).

Fig. 7. *The Purification of the Leper*. Fresco by Botticelli in the Sistine Chapel (cf. Plate 17).

Fig. 8. *The Annunciation*. Fresco by Botticelli (from San Martino). Florence, Belvedere (cf. Plate 14).

Fig. 9. *A Miracle of St. Zenobius and his Death*. Painting by Botticelli. Dresden, Gallery (cf. Plate 47).

Fig. 10. *A Miracle of St. Zenobius*. Painting by Botticelli. London, National Gallery (cf. Plate 48).

remained on a wall in the Villa Lemmi, shows scanty fragments of an old man in a red robe, a small girl, a parapet with a Persian carpet and a river landscape behind.

All that is certain about the subject-matter of the Lemmi frescoes is summed up in the captions to Plates 22 and 23; the rest is pure speculation.

26–27. *Madonna of the Magnificat*. Panel, 46½ in. diameter. Florence, Uffizi.

This picture, one of the most popular that Botticelli ever painted, is very badly preserved. Three old copies (the best known of which is in the Louvre) show some changes in the composition: the angel behind the two boys on the left has wings; the other angel at the left, of whom only the head and one arm are visible in the Uffizi picture, does not appear at all in the copies, where the crown is held only by the angel at the right; the round window with the view of a landscape is simpler in the copies. The picture will need further and thorough examination before it is possible to decide how far bad restoration and overpainting are responsible for its present appearance.

The text in the open book reads: *Magnificat anima mea dominum et exsultavit spiritus meus in Deo* (Luke i, 46 f.). The first word of this hymn has given the picture its name. Bode has dated it correctly about 1485.

28. *Mars and Venus*. Panel, 27¼×68¼ in. London, National Gallery.

Gombrich has proved that the picture was painted for a member of the Vespucci family, whose emblem, the wasps, appears above the head of Mars. The meaning of the allegory can be summed up in the words: *When love is awake, discord sleeps*. The small satyrs, half men and half goats, cannot arouse the god of war, who remains deaf even to the sound of the shell trumpet; not even the satyr who raises himself up under the sleeper's arm, nor the wasps whose stings can hurt like desires of the senses, awaken the God of War, the counterpart of *Humanitas*. (When Lucretius invokes Venus, the goddess of peace, to assist him in his work, he asks her "Cause meanwhile the savage works of war to sleep and be still over every sea and land.")

Botticelli's *Mars and Venus*, cleaned in 1943, is very well preserved. Only the gold in the hair and robe of Venus (our reproductions of this and other pictures are printed without gold) has been largely renewed.

29–30. *The Birth of Venus*. Canvas, 67⅞×109⅝ in. Florence, Uffizi.

Horne has proved that the picture was painted for Lorenzo and Giovanni di Pierfrancesco de' Medici.

The birth of Venus is linked with the myth of Earth and Heaven. When heaven, in the darkness of night, embraced the earth and was deprived of his manhood, foam appeared on the sea and from it rose Venus, the goddess of loving desire and perpetual beauty. Driven by the west wind, she glides over the waves in a shell and steps on land when she reaches the island of Cythera. In Paphos the Seasons, or Horae, wrap her in garments.

Horne has noted that the picture is much less well preserved than the *Primavera*, because the unvarnished tempera colours had faded; that it shows only few retouches, but has suffered through overcleaning; that the colours at the left edge, around the feet of the wind gods, have been damaged by damp; and that the right arm of Venus has been overpainted and its outline changed. In spite of these damages, the picture may be described as well preserved.

31–32. *Madonna and Child with the two Saints John*. Panel, 72⅞×70⅞ in. Berlin-Dahlem, Museum.

The picture was originally in the Bardi Chapel of the Church of Santo Spirito in Florence, and was still there when Vasari saw it. According to documents published by Supino, Giuliano da Sangallo received payment for the frame in February 1485 and Botticelli six months later for the painting.

The picture is well preserved, apart from slight damages and retouchings.

33–34. *Madonna of the Pomegranate*. Panel, 56¼ in. diameter. Florence, Uffizi.

Probably identical with a tondo, mentioned in the documents, which Botticelli painted in 1487 for the "Audience Chamber" in the Palazzo Vecchio, a court of appellate jurisdiction. The identification of this picture with the tondo of 1487 was first suggested by Horne and was later accepted by Adolfo Venturi, Berenson and Mesnil.

The pomegranate (here held by the Virgin and by the Child) is a symbol of varying significance. According to Horne it signifies the Fall of Man; another explanation connects it with the sacrificial Death and Resurrection of Christ; in Antiquity it was an attribute of Proserpine and, because of its numerous seeds, a symbol of immortality. Later it came to symbolize the Christian Church as enclosing countless seeds in one fruit.

The picture is still in its original frame and is well preserved, but in need of cleaning.

35. *Dante*. Canvas, 20⅝×15¾ in. Cologny-Geneva, Dr. Martin Bodmer collection.

This portrait has frequently been reproduced (Bode, Adolfo Venturi, Gamba), but always without the stone frame around the window. Apparently the picture was judged from photographs, and this painted surround was believed to be the actual frame. Mesnil (page 223) was mistaken in calling the picture "much overpainted".

From about 1890 onwards, this Dante portrait had been in England, in the collections of Alfred Seymour, London; Langton Douglas, London; and Mrs. Burns, Hatfield. In 1931 it was sold to Switzerland.

The date of the picture is uncertain. It is generally dated about 1495, but it seems to have been painted about the same time as the portraits of the Popes in the Vatican (1481).

36. *Illustration to Dante's Divine Comedy*. Body-colour on parchment. 12¾×18¾ in. Berlin, Print Room.

In 1481 an edition of Dante with a commentary by Cristoforo Landino and nineteen engravings to the first nineteen cantos of the *Inferno* was published in Florence.

These illustrations, which had been engraved with indifferent success in the workshop of Baccio Baldini, are reproductions of drawings by Botticelli. He illustrated only nineteen out of the one hundred cantos of the *Divina Commedia*, and left the work unfinished when he went to Rome to start work on the frescoes of the Sistine Chapel.

More than ten years later, Botticelli began once more to illustrate the *Divina Commedia*. Large parchment sheets were bound as a codex, the left-hand pages being reserved for the text, which was written out in a beautiful antiqua script, and the right-hand pages for Botticelli's drawings. The Anonimo Gaddiano records that this Dante manuscript had been commissioned by Lorenzo di Pierfrancesco de' Medici, who also owned the three finest of Botticelli's allegories, the *Primavera*, the *Birth of Venus* and *Mars and Venus*.

Ninety-three of Botticelli's Dante illustrations are still extant (85 in Berlin and 8 in the Vatican Library). Only three of them are finished in colour; the others are monochrome: prepared with soft metal-point, and gone over with pen and ink. Since the pen drawings show a lightness of touch and elegance of line which are lost when the drawings are coloured, it has been suggested that the colouring was discontinued because the first few attempts proved disappointing. But such a preference for the sketch is not in keeping with the taste of the Renaissance, and it can hardly be doubted that all of Botticelli's Dante drawings were intended to be coloured. I think, however, that it was not Botticelli himself, but a miniaturist who was to finish the illustrations in colour.

From 1495 to 1497 Botticelli seems to have worked almost exclusively for Lorenzo di Pierfrancesco, for whom he decorated two villas with frescoes. The Dante drawings for Lorenzo were made most probably during the same period. From 1491 onwards, Botticelli had been working on the mosaics of the Zanobi Chapel in the Cathedral of Florence, together with the miniaturist Gherardo di Giovanni. I believe that the colouring of the three finished drawings can be ascribed to Gherardo, who died in 1497, and that owing to his early death nearly all of Botticelli's Dante drawings remained monochrome.

Plate 36 illustrates the eighteenth canto of the Inferno, which describes the punishment of procurers, seducers and flatterers in the eighth circle of Hell (called *Malebolge* or the evil chasms). In this drawing (as in the fresco of the Youth of Moses, repr. page 12) Botticelli makes use of the so-called continuous representation, which in his time had already gone out of fashion. Several incidents are combined in one picture, scene follows scene as on a revolving stage. Here Dante and Virgil appear six times, making their way from left to right around the edge of the crater.

37. *The Lamentation over Christ*. Panel, $55\frac{1}{8} \times 81\frac{1}{2}$ in. Munich, State Gallery.
According to Mesnil, the picture comes from the monastery of San Paolino in Florence and was restored at the Uffizi in 1873. It is by Botticelli's own hand, but a part of the surface has been rubbed off by the restorer.

38. *Madonna under a Baldachin*. Panel, $25\frac{5}{8}$ in. diameter. Milan, Ambrosiana.
Horne and Gamba identify this tondo with a picture which Vasari mentions as being in the (no longer extant) monastery Santa Maria degli Angioli in Florence.
The painting is very well preserved.

39. *St. Augustine in his Cell*. Panel, 17×11 in. Florence, Uffizi.
The present reproduction is the first to show the *complete* painting: without the modern frame, which covers too much at the edges, particularly at the bottom.
Botticelli has incised the perspective construction very carefully into the gesso priming with a stylus; this construction is visible through the curtain and the verticals of the architecture extend to the lower edge of the picture.
Horne has pointed to a certain technical similarity of this small painting to miniatures by Gherardo di Giovanni. This miniaturist collaborated with Botticelli on the mosaics of the Zanobi Chapel in the Cathedral of Florence (1491-1494) and, if my theory is correct, was entrusted by him with the colouring of the Dante drawings (1496-1497). Gamba has dated the *St. Augustine* about 1495.

40. *The Annunciation*. Panel, $59 \times 51\frac{3}{8}$ in. Florence, Uffizi.
According to a document published by Milanesi, the picture was commissioned by a certain Benedetto Guardi as altarpiece for a chapel in the Church of Santa Maria Maddalena de' Pazzi. Botticelli had started work on March 19, 1489, and the chapel was consecrated in the following year.
The painting was executed in Botticelli's workshop, and the collaboration of Filippino Lippi can be recognized, particularly in the landscape. The painting is in perfect condition and is still in the original frame.

41. *The Lamentation over Christ*. Panel, 42×28 in. Milan, Poldi Pezzoli Museum.
This picture is identified almost generally with a *Pietà* which, according to Vasari, was in the Church of Santa Maria Maggiore in Florence.
The painting was cleaned in 1951 and is well preserved.

42. *The Calumny of Apelles*. Panel, $24\frac{3}{8} \times 35\frac{3}{4}$ in. Florence, Uffizi.
Painted for Antonio Segni, who also employed Leonardo da Vinci. The picture is very well preserved.
Apelles, the most celebrated painter of Antiquity and portraitist of Alexander the Great, had painted an "Allegory of Calumny", which was known to the humanists from a description by Lucian and which several Renaissance painters, among them Mantegna and Dürer, had tried to reconstruct. In Botticelli's painting, King Ptolemy is seen seated on his throne. Folly and Suspicion whisper into his ears and before him stands Envy in ragged clothes. Calumny drags along the victim of a false accusation, Guile and Deceit weave flowers into Calumny's hair to make her even more attractive than she already is. Repentance follows far behind, in mourning garb, and turns round to look at

Truth, who stands naked and motionless, pointing to heaven.

43. *The Tragedy of Lucretia.* Panel, 33½×70½ in. Boston, Isabella Stewart Gardner Museum.

The painting combines several incidents from the history of Lucretia: at the left, Lucretia resisting the assault of Tarquinius; at the right, Lucretia's suicide; in the centre, Lucretia's body on the bier and the revolt of the people. (See Livy, i, 57-60.)

The picture is much better preserved than its pendant in Bergamo.

44. *Mystic Nativity.* Canvas, 42¾×29½ in. London, National Gallery.

The Greek inscription at the top reads in translation: *I, Sandro, painted this picture at the end of the year 1500 during the tribulations of Italy in the half time after the time, in accordance with the eleventh Chapter of St. John in the second woe of the Apocalypse, during the unchaining of the devil for three and a half years; then he will be fettered in accordance with the twelfth Chapter, as in this picture.*

This is the only picture by Botticelli which is both signed and dated. In ancient Florence, the year began on March 25, the Feast of the Annunciation. "At the end of the year 1500" means therefore, according to our calendar, March 1501.

The inscription, which has been interpreted repeatedly, but never satisfactorily, cannot be proved to refer to the martyrdom of Savonarola and his two companions on May 23, 1498. In March 1501, Florence was afflicted by war, the plague and internal troubles (see the Diary of Luca Landucci, ed. Marie Herzfeld, 1913, pages 54-57). The "tribulations of Italy" refer perhaps, as has been suggested repeatedly, to Cesare Borgia and the French invasion of Northern Italy. The picture is rubbed, but free from overpainting.

45. *The Agony in the Garden.* Panel, 20⅞×13¾ in. Granada, Royal Chapel.

First published by Gomez Moreno (*Gazette des Beaux-Arts*, 1908). The picture is certainly older than the funerary chapel of the Spanish kings in Granada (built, according to Enrique de Egas, after 1504). It was painted about the same time as the "Mystic Crucifixion" now in the Fogg Art Museum, Cambridge, Mass. (1501-1502).

46. *Judith.* Panel, 14¼×7¾ in. Amsterdam, Rijksmuseum.

Published first by Frizzoni (1902). The picture belonged to Edwin vom Rath and entered the Rijksmuseum in 1941 after his death. When it was freed from overpaintings, the damaged figure of the servant on the right came to light. Some parts of the picture are well preserved.

47-48. *Scenes from the Life of St. Zenobius.* Panels, Dresden, Gallery; and London, National Gallery.

The two details, in about one third of the original size, are taken from two of the paintings reproduced complete on page 76. The full series comprises four panels: two in the National Gallery, London; one in the Metropolitan Museum, New York; and one in the Dresden Gallery. The four pictures show the life, the miracles and the death of St. Zenobius, bishop of Florence (who died about 1100 years before Botticelli's time).

Our two plates show St. Zenobius raising dead children to life and restoring them to their mothers.

The paintings are well preserved.

Colour plates in the Introduction:

I. *Self-Portrait of Botticelli.* Detail from Plate 12.
II. *Flora.* Detail from Plate 10.

LIST OF COLLECTIONS